# CHRIST Revealed in You

## The Hope of Glory

By Diane Cordaire

*Diane Cordaire!*

Christ Revealed in You, The Hope of Glory
PRINTED 2023
dianecordaire@gmail.com
www.1mob1god.com
ISBN: 978-0-9943740-5-9

# ABOUT THE AUTHOUR

In the beginning, my biography in my first book was lengthy and self-centred. Now I have a clear understanding of my identity in Christ. It feels as if my previous life and my current life are in completely separate worlds, never to meet again. The skills acquired along the way stay and are used in a way beyond my hopes or understanding for His purpose, not mine. God says build my house and I will build yours. The boundaries between what I considered my life and God's life blurred together and became one along the way. There's only one life worth talking about, and it's His. God, the Father, summoned us all, but not everyone heeded the call. In this book, I share some stories of how I reached this point of oneness and the process of understandings that came with this journey. In the first three books I have separated the scriptures out of the writing. This method kept me checking on myself to make sure I was speaking His word with accuracy. I noticed a different thing happened whilst writing this book. The scriptures merged into the writing, and I became one with the writer. The series of books written illustrates the way out of oneself and into the One who called us.

I call it the overcoming process. It is necessary to overcome oneself to see Him who called us by name.

Knowing me isn't what you need. The importance lies in the content of the writings. Knowing you is what truly matters! Once you uncover yourself, you discover Christ in you.

The hope of glory!

The simple things in life we often miss!

# FORWARD

We are seated with God in Christ! Everything is conveyed in this scripture. By being in Christ, we can contribute to the bringing of His Kingdom to the earth. We have been equipped for a time such as this. This book is the fourth in a series I wrote about overcoming my sinful nature to become Christ-like on earth. The days that are upon the earth will require individuals who embody the power and authority of our Lord Jesus Christ with His vision for earth. The purpose of these books is to direct everyone towards Christ, in whom we find hope and glory. To become who you were always born to become.

We were meant to be Christ's reflection on earth, but Satan's disruptive temptations of sin caused our reflection to become unclear. This book, along with my other books, directs you towards Christ's face. The hope that leads to glory! His face mirrors your face. You will shine with His righteousness and be covered in His glory.

I hope you see what I've seen through the following writings:

Previous books include:
- How I Overcame my own Life
- Born to Be Holy
- Resurrection, Glorification and His Kingdom is HERE

To receive what I have obtained is to see Christ alive in you! And Miracles, Signs and Wonders will follow those who believe. That seems like a good title for the next book. Enjoy the revelations and understandings that emerge from these writings.

## CHAPTER 1

## CROSSING OVER

*You rescued me from my enemies and set me in a broad place.*

I kiss the feet of the King and my heart leaps with joy as I spy out the land of promise!

To follow the King of Glory is the journey of a faithful believer. Many receive an invitation, but only a few are elected for this great and mighty task. I abandoned the conveniences of society to trek across the desert, similar to Moses' journey with the Israelites. The Holy Spirit was my guide and comforter. Those lifeless places called deserts were within me and had to be overcome. Anticipating the day, the promises would be fulfilled. After a twelve-year journey with no other human by my side, I triumphed over my fears. After many years of determination, perseverance, dedication, and endurance, I stood at the edge of my own desert, peering into what had been promised by Him, who led me through my fears and dry places. Taking that long-awaited step onto the land was inspiring, but only for a moment. What I witnessed was what the seven spies observed when Moses sent them. Giants ruling the land! What report will I return with?

Initially, it looked like I failed this test until I noticed that these giants weren't giants at all. The waiting to cross over into the promised land was also a test. Would I hit the rock as Moses had and lose patience with the Lord? Believers who walk in faith are trained to wait on the Lord. Our transformed behaviour waits for the Lord's unction before we move. Timing is everything! It's a dance with the Divine. If you proceed without His unction, the flow of the Spirit stops. This stopping sets us right and readjusts us with His Spirit. God's desire is your desire. There is only one!

The journey across the river Jordan is a river within our own soul. Our body is composed of dust and earth, this is our land. I always said my mind is heaven and my body is earth. Bringing heaven to earth has always been the plan. This is achieved in the mind and body first before it manifests in the physical realm. The crossing of this river produces an understanding and revelation like no other. It's like a spark igniting! A bride and her groom crossing the threshold together. New life springs forth. It's another mystery of Christ within.

When Joshua moved across the Jordan river, the priest stepped into the water with the Ark of the Covenant and the water stopped flowing. That's faith! It is necessary to take that same step to reach our promised land. The water caused a build-up at a town up stream called Adam. The definition of Adam is 'death'. The heaped-up water also hit another town called Zarethan, which means, 'piercing, bleeding of the veins'. 'Go down' is the equivalent term for Jordan. Death and the piercing of the veins give the impression that Jesus Christ and God the Father were at the crossing long before we ever dipped our toe into this river. This is the gateway for the Ark of the Covenant (Glory) and man to become one, the fullness of salvation. We have left behind judgement and death in the barren desert. And the blood of Jesus Christ cleansed us as we came through the cross of Calvary and overcame our fallen nature.

The Glory that takes us into the promises is not the cloud that led us through the desert - it's the Glory that rests on our shoulders. The priests carried the Ark over the Jordan; the Glory rested upon their shoulders. We are taking our Lord into His land by becoming one with Him. It's the unity of humans and God. And the two are united to become one. His dreams are His vision for His Kingdom on earth.

While journeying over the river, the advisers instructed twelve leaders, one from each tribe, to pick up a large stone from the middle of the riverbed. They moved the stones eight miles to the town of Gilgal and placed the stones as a memorial to remember what God had done. Twelve represents divine government, and the stones were carried on their shoulders, which is in alignment with the scripture, "the Government will rest upon His shoulders." We are His governing authority, and we reign with Him. The Israelites passed through the river as a united force, with one heart, one mind, and one vision. Guided by the Glory, they walked past the Ark, which was being carried by the priest in the middle of the river. The people had never been next to the Ark. Back then, it was only the priests who went into the Holy of Holies where the Ark was kept. In the desert, they followed the cloud of God's Glory by day and the pillar of fire by night. This crossing is showing that there is a shift occurring, the Israelites will bring His presence into the promised land.

Once the Israelites were on the opposite bank of the river, the Canaanites from Jericho had heard of the river parting and were worried at what was coming towards them. Our timing is not the same as God's timing! If we were leading, we would have moved forward on Jericho when we felt our strongest. Making our way across a divided river on dry land would have made us feel brave and powerful. God commanded the Israelites to circumcise themselves, which weakened them for battle. The message I received from that act was, God is capable of winning battles without using our flesh.

Once circumcised, they consumed their first food in the new land. That nourishment wasn't a heavenly provision called manna, as they were accustomed to in the desert. It was crops and fruits from Canaan. The desert manna was dispersed like bread fragments from the heavens every day. Manna symbolized Christ, the bread of life. He said eat this bread and remember me! It is evident once again that Jesus Christ was in spirit form, but He hadn't come to earth in the flesh body yet. The fresh food from the promised land was grain, which represents resurrected life.

To permit God to guide us towards a new diet for life, we must abandon our past desert way of life and the way we used to be fed. This upcoming Joshua Generation will work, labour, and sweat in the dirt to bring in the harvest. They brought the keys of David into the reality of today. They are the ambassadors of God on earth. They evolved into the manna from heaven, with Christ in them as the hope of Glory! The newly established government with a shared inheritance with Christ as the cornerstone. The new Jerusalem!

The Commander of the Angel Armies visited Joshua before the battle in Jericho occurred. Joshua was told by the Lord to remove his sandals, for he was standing on holy ground, just like God had said to Moses. What the Lord communicated to Joshua is your standing in the battle's victory. "Your faith is the victory, and I, the Lord God, have granted Jericho to you."

They firmly locked the gates of Jericho since the Canaanites knew about the Israelites' coming and were filled with fear. The Lord announced the battle was won before they fought the battle. Realizing that we can count on the victory because the Lord God has already ordained the final outcome. Our Lord finished His work with complete triumph over everything, including death. God's side of the equation has been finished for a long time. Our stance, which is our disbelief, needs to match His conquest. 'IT IS DONE', are the well-known words of our Lord, and these words ring true here.

In the past, we have documented our plans and asked the Lord to bless them or shut the door on the plan if it wasn't His will. Joshua's approach was to ask the Lord for His plan. It would have been a shock to Joshua when the Lord instructed them to march around the city once a day for seven days and blow their shofars. Joshua followed orders, as did all the other Israelites. The priests carried the Ark of the Covenant as they circled around the city. The priests were stationed with shofars in front of the Israelites, and more priests with shofars were stationed at the rear, forming the final line. The march was in unity! The Canaanites inside the city would have been confused by this war strategy.

But Joshua obeyed what the Lord of the Angel Armies had commanded. When the walls tumbled, they fell forward, not inward. It was the blast from heaven that made the walls crumble. They marched as a collective unit with the Lord towards victory, even though they may not have comprehended the tactical plan of the battle the Lord had given them. It was the sound of celebration in faith that caused heaven to move, and the walls came tumbling down. Those walls are in us! It's our disbelief we're asking heaven to eradicate. Our cries of triumph in faith demolishes those barriers. Everything is achievable with Our Lord at the helm.

What level of effort are you prepared to put into breaking down those walls and reclaiming what is rightfully yours? When the Lord manifests, victory is inevitable. Heaven's glory is manifested on earth when your victory proclamation aligns with God's words. When the walls came down the Israelites rushed up and in and took the city. Pay attention, it says run up! The walls collapsing outward resulted in an ascent and they ran up and in. God created it easy; all they had to do was not use their flesh and circle the city and run up and in. Amazing! Jericho and all the idols, including their wheat, were set on fire. All the remaining things were offered with complete loyalty to the Lord. It's important that we dedicate all goods to our Lord and His treasury once we take our promise land. If we don't, it will act against us!

Let's recap what brought the walls down. Partnership in obedience to God, with faith and a shout of rejoicing, brought the walls crashing down. It wasn't by works of the flesh. Apparently, when the men marched around the city, they didn't say a word, not one word for seven days until that shout of victory came rushing out. That's unity! Partnership in faith with the Lord of Hosts and His Angel Army brought victory. You don't have to win the battle - you only have to stand in the battle's victory. And that battle is within you to overcome your walls. Then you will be led into the promise.

Based on what I've witnessed in life, God uses the foolish things to confound the wise. What seemed like a foolish plan confounded the Canaanites and Jericho became the victory. The walls of Jericho were constructed with an inner and outer wall that was very thick. The external wall was 30ft tall and 6ft wide, the internal wall was 30ft tall and 12ft wide. They steered chariots around the top. Huge walls, get the picture? It wasn't the Israelites marching or making noise that brought those walls down. The Lord of Promises commanded the army of Angels to push those walls out. Complete takeover and reclaiming of what rightfully belongs to the Lord and His people. The Lord will recover His inheritance that each of us holds. Once retrieved, it will be devoted back to Him.

There was one partition that remained standing in Jericho, and that was the divider where Rahab and her family were commanded to remain. Rahab concealed the spies from the Canaanites when they went to spy out the land. Rahab was informed about Moses crossing the desert and the sea parting. Her status as a prostitute made her the least important in everyone's eyes. But in God's eyes, He only saw her bravery in faith to hide the spies. Rahab didn't receive any formal education in theology. She had faith like a mustard seed, and that was enough for her to believe in the living God. Rahab and her family were spared from harm when the walls came crashing down. Her marital status was unmarried, and she had no offspring. Her family was Mum, Dad and siblings. Eventually, she became the wife of a Hebrew man and had a son named Boaz, who later united in marriage with Ruth. King David's ancestry traces back to this family line. Rahab was elevated to the position of the great- great grandmother of King David. God uses the foolish to baffle the wise. All He requires is faith.

When we triumph, often we gain confidence, and pride creeps in. The Lord commanded Joshua to take the next town, which was Ai. Joshua stated they wouldn't need to send all the soldiers, just three thousand men. Joshua was positioned in his confident, prideful place and didn't even send the Ark of God into this battle with the soldiers. The men of 'Ai' ran after and killed some of the Israelites outside of their town. The disobedience and pride that came into them prevented the Lord from giving them that battle. Don't underestimate the Lord's role in achieving victory in battles. Joshua's experience provides a valuable lesson. Obeying the Lord's command is more crucial than shifting without the Ark of Glory. Joshua repented and tore his clothes once he heard what had occurred. Don't repeat Joshua's error as we enter our promise land to possess our inheritance with the Lord.

The Lord revealed to Joshua, who had sinned within the community. His name was Achan, and he had stolen a robe, 200 pieces of silver and a wedge of gold. Joshua probed him for an explanation. Achan answered, "I saw, wanted, and I took." Achan repented, but they took him with his tent and livestock to a valley called 'Trouble'. The definition of 'Achan' in Hebrew is 'Trouble'. The complete camp of a million Israelites was affected by one man's disobedience to the Lord's command. We will not experience everything the Lord has for us until we obey and let go of all the desires of the flesh. Achan impacted everyone! Everything we do has consequences on all who are associated with the decisions you make or don't make. We are to be the beacon of His Glory and take back all that belongs to God. Keeping anything that belongs to God will surely bring destruction upon our lives and the surrounding people.

Advancing to additional battles, Joshua did it differently next time. He abstained from proceeding until the Lord's strategies were provided.

There is a divine battle to reclaim all that is of the Kingdom, and it starts with us. Ask yourself if any of these following disturbances describe you or the territory you have been asked to reclaim.

1. **The Hittites** - Terrorist, broken into piece, self-protection.
2. **The Amorites** - Pride, arrogance, sense of superior and self-Worship
3. **The Canaanites** - Merchant, pirates or traffickers. Materialism and the love of money. Vanity and worthless distractions
4. **The Perizzites** - Rustic country dwellers or country folk. Lacking vision and stuck in tradition. Loyal to the old rusty ways. Looking backwards into the old. Fear of change and fear of man.
5. **The Hivite** - Serpent who lays out in order the schemes of the enemy.
6. **The Jebusites** - Trodden down, conquered and subdued, depression.

7. **The Girgashites** - Dense, dull, Ignorant
8. **The Gibeonites** - Live in the hills with lies of spiritual power not of God.

---

Over a prolonged time, I endeavoured to fulfil the promise that's written on my DNA. Every attempt I made ended in failure, but with each attempt, I came closer to conquering my ambition and divided vision in my fallen nature. If the human understanding can convince you to give up on what has been assigned to you by our Lord, then you lose your purpose. Imagine reuniting with our Heavenly Father at the end of time with that truth. Where once was the promise written of His Kingdom, you didn't receive it on earth. No Thanks! It wasn't about giving up on the purpose and promise; it was about grasping how God performs things and how His procedures differ from ours. The beauty of living is in the learning. Another possibility to carry out the assigned task has emerged for me. At this moment, I'm waiting for Him to move every piece into play so the promise will be given as the gift as foretold. "Sovereign Lord, you are God". Your covenant is trustworthy, and you have promised these good things to your servant. Now be pleased to bless the house of your servant. That I may continue forever in your sight. For, you, Sovereign Lord, have spoken and with your blessing, the house of your servant will be blessed forever" (2 Samuel 7:25-29). Unless we embrace all elements of the covenant, it cannot be executed.

Whenever I triumph over a fragment of my being, the manifestation of God's vision draws nearer to being established on this earth. Seek His face and all else will be added. By seeking, we gain knowledge and by gaining knowledge, we put into practice what He teaches us. Faith without actions is lifeless. The Lord says to build His house, and He will build your house and bless your family. Many individuals have this scripture around the wrong way. They are shaping their destiny and hopefully there is ample time for the Lord after they have finished. Incorrect direction, turn around and rethink your approach. That's self-centred thinking. The Lord communicates by telling us to follow Him and leave behind everything. "Direct your gaze towards Me and My Kingdom," says the Lord.

I have arrived at a good place on this journey, and it's not due to my intelligence. The Lord takes advantage of the people who come last. Why would God use those who are last? Because those who are trailing behind know how to seek His will, His face, and His hand. They have been humbled to trust in the Lord and lean not on their own understandings. This humble position causes His plan to be established. "Come into my courts with thanksgiving and praise." The courts are where we bring our requests before the Lord. What I've noticed over my pilgrimage with the Lord is that polluted bloodlines can obstruct us from achieving the promises on this earth. The bloodline carries the burden of ancestral sins, leading to delays that can span up to and beyond ten generations. As soon as we step foot in the courts of our Lord and confess our hereditary sins before Him, we will be liberated from polluted blood ties. Satan's power over your promises can be eliminated if you don't provide him with an opening.

Many times, those openings come from our past ancestors.

To step into His presence on earth, we must surpass our knowledge. At the time I wrote my earlier works, His word was not yet fully integrated into my writing. Nowadays, His words are merged into one voice and one word within my body. By stepping up, we will embody His presence, and others can witness His righteousness and glory through us. Move closer and enter His intimacy! That's the step of faith needed to progress. That has been the aim all along, while competing in the race set out before us. His righteousness will radiate from within us, which is His glory resting on our shoulders, the Ark of His Glory. We are the dwelling place of the living God on earth. A regenerated people completely healed and throbbing with the presence of our living God. The establishment of The New Jerusalem is based on Jesus Christ as the cornerstone, and we've been transformed to appear as living stones.

This present day is preparing for the emergence of a new governing body. Those who are observant will recognise His Kingdom and this new governing body. These people have been instructed to be those who bring justice upon the earth. This modern generation is no better than the ones before the great flood in Noah's era. As in the day of Noah, so it will be in our day before the appearance of the Son of man. We are the heritage of Christ, Our Lord, His favoured bride. God has designated an inheritance for us to take back. In simpler terms, He resides within us, and we exist within Him as a single entity. What has been foreordained is written in the book of life. We are His magnificent body walking on the earth and all the earth is His. Reclaiming land, atmospheres, and authority, just as Joshua did, is what the task is all about. Function as the assistant who is attentive to your Father's work, thus, when Christ returns, you will be noticed nurturing the household of our Father. That implies taking care of God's people.

The plans of the enemy are finally being exposed as the selfish ambition of man. They think there is no God, no spirit, and we have no free will. Technology has infiltrated the mind of man, and it has become their God. That's the abomination of the desolation. The Lord declares that when we see the abomination of desolation set up in the holy place, that's when He is at the door, ready for the return. People are sacred beings and the Holy Spirit lives within them. The establishment of technology as a replacement for the Holy Spirit in man is an abomination and idolatry. The aim of these days is for individuals to come together and repent and return to the living God.

We must recover all that has been stolen with the false authority of man's mind. Our Lord declared that it was done. So, position yourself where God positions Himself in the fulfillment of everything. The human brain assumes it's the master, but it's a rebellion against God's will. The mind of man is declining and will keep declining. Out of the carcass of man will come something sweet. Everything that God intends to establish will be achieved through the prayers of the saints. Stand up and start moving towards your part of His Kingdom. Our rivals are noisy in war, but our conflict is not against physical entities, it is against powers and principalities. The spirit realm possesses both powers and principalities.

That's where our fight starts and ends. It's where His Kingdom is manifested on earth. His Kingdom and this birth right abide in you.

The serpent that whispered to Eve in the garden will attempt to convince you out of your inheritance. Step on that serpent and crush it! I encountered that incident recently where I crushed the python spirit with my heel. I also felt myself hauling the dragon over the barren desert with a chain around its neck and tossing it into the abyss and locking it up for a thousand years. If we are not enraged enough to overthrow all the obstacles in our path as we move ahead, then we haven't made enough headway to manifest His Kingdom on earth. It's the violent who takes the Kingdom by storm! In my experience with the Lord, it's when I've had enough, and I pull heaven to earth. Enough is enough! Today is that day, there is no other day like today. Fasting, prayer, and worship opens the heavens. What are you waiting for? Get violent and pull your answer out of heaven. Every good gift comes under grace. Call upon God's angels to bring this good news under His grace. Amen!

To take back what has been stolen from our Lord. It's the beginning of a new life and day. We don't wrestle against flesh and blood, but against spiritual wickedness and strongholds in the spirit realm. These strongholds transpire into the natural realm if you don't tackle them in the spirit realm. Often, I see people tackling their battles in the natural realm before the spiritual realm. It's the wrong way around.

CHAPTER 2

# WHAT IS HIDDEN MANNA?

*Christ!* That's our hidden treasure. And that treasure is in YOU!

I am the living bread which came down from heaven. He who eats My flesh and drinks My blood abides in Me, and I in him. As the living Father sent Me, and I live because of the Father, so he who feeds on Me will live because of Me [John 6:51].

The followers of Christ are headed for restoration - resurrected bodies. Heaven and earth, an ordered construction that accommodates two distinct domains with a single common goal. The writer of Hebrews explains that the earthly tabernacle was a "copy and shadow of the heavenly things."

## Jesus Alive in Us

The hidden manna is Jesus Christ in us on earth as it is in heaven. He is the treasured inheritance, and we are His treasured inheritance. He is who we seek. He is undying, and immortality blended. Let's take a walk and reveal the presence of our risen Lord, now on earth, in a glorified human form as it is in heaven.

We, His people, are His temple on the earth. God designed Eden to mirror the heavenly sanctuary with man and woman as the temple. Far from being two independent realms, God designed earth to mirror heavenly realities. Genesis reflects this as a marriage covenant. An earthly picture of the heavenly reality, God's relationship with His people.

Eden's garden-sanctuary not only reflects the heavenly sanctuary, but it is also an access point between heaven and earth—a place where the two realms occupy the same space. Adam, in relationship with Yahweh, enjoys His heavenly presence. Eden was placed on a mountain and in this mountain sanctuary, heaven, and earth overlap. The two realms co-exist as God dwells both in heaven and on earth with His people. In the beginning, God created the heavens and the earth. But the end goal of creation is the restoration of heaven with earth and man with God once again.

"And they heard the voice of the LORD God walking in the garden in the cool of the day: and Adam and his wife hid themselves from the presence of the LORD God amongst the trees of the garden" (Genesis 3:8).

That verse is the curse! Hiding themselves from the Lord's presence. This is the place that the Lord has been getting us to so He can reverse the curse. "Let your presence be seen onceagain," is the cry of our hearts.

The dividing question?

So if anyone tells you, 'There He is, out in the desert,' do not go out; or, 'Here He is, in the inner rooms,' do not believe it. For as lightning that comes from the east is visible even in the west, so will be the coming of the Son of Man [Luke 17:23].

For years, people have gone running to conventions and events held by the communities of good, intended people. Why? To see Jesus. But He wasn't there. Even the great revivals didn't last. They faded out. Why? Because the Glory that entered the room was separate from the people who hosted the revivals. Christ, the Holy Spirit, and the Father are not separate from you. He is you, but you have forgotten you are Christ alive, so we operate like He is separate and has to come into a room. The revivals of the past got fearful that they couldn't contain the move of God and they stopped the flow. You can't contain God. God is breaking all containments NOW. Church buildings, mission field are all being broken open so the spirit of the Lord can flow in and around His people.

This next move will see Christ in a people who will not fade away. Christ in them the hope of Glory. There is no separation from the love of God. The Glory will not depart this time.

Immortal beings on an earthy journey.

"God created mankind in his own image, in the image of God He created them; male and female He created them" [Genesis 1:27].

This statement is given while still in the garden. Man's mind agreed with God's mind, and they walked in the garden in the cool part of the day. Note their mental alignment. The path changed when man's 'free will' ate from the tree of knowledge of good and evil. As a result, all of us ended up in the tree of knowledge of good and evil. I have always expressed that we are not free until our 'will' is in 'His will'. Everything outside 'His will' is rebellion or the tree of knowledge of good and evil.

We carry the essence of immortality. At the start was the Word, and the Word was with God and the Word was God. The divine became flesh and dwells within us. (John 1-14). When we hit the end of ourselves, that's when Christ can raise up within our temple (body). We need to reintegrate our mindfulness with the living Christ within us to surpass being simply a human in a man's or woman's physicality. To showcase God's glorified form, we need to connect with God's image and physical existence prior to the fall of humanity.

We entered the realm of mortality, but you will rise out of death to wear the divine, resurrected, glorified body. Our fallen nature identified with the tree of knowledge of good and evil instead of the resurrected Christ within. Life's expedition was to recognise all that was false from the fallen tree and choose life over death. As individuals who belong to the Body of Christ, we need to hold Christ as the head and mature into the head.

You are the Christ described in scripture. You are the embodiment of Christ on earth as it is in heaven. And we are His special possession. God's love transcends all boundaries, there is no separation. We are one body, one mind and one spirit. When we step into Christ's reality, we can become more than an average human walking the earth. When Jesus ascended, He gave us the Holy Spirit, our comforter. The Divine Spirit lives in us as a part of the Trinity. That connects us with the Father, and Son. We are His spirit upon the earth. The LORD God formed a man from the dust of the ground and blew into his nostrils the breath of life, and the man became a living being (Genesis 2:7). We are His being, the real embodiment of His hope. Now faith is the substance of things hoped for, the evidence of things not seen. By faith, we understand the Word of God framed the worlds. Our faith helps us to comprehend the profound things of God that the Lord is revealing to us. It would be hard for individuals who haven't undergone this transformation to believe we are Christ's representation on the earth. Not by works, but by the Spirit. It is written in the Holy scriptures, "We are ambassadors of Christ." His image on earth. That's all I need to realise the truth, and the truth sets us free. It's beyond my understanding and that makes it right for me to take hold of this truth.

Christ - the power, the wisdom, and the glory of God - is buried in us and will be raised in us. Love is the human form raised and recognised as divine.

The identity of God! All the prophets of God agreed to the identity and nature of God. God said to Moses, "I AM WHO I AM." This is what you are to say to the Israelites, "I AM has sent me to you."

We cannot partake of two trees if we want our free will to be wholly surrendered to the Lord. There are two trees: the tree of knowledge of good and evil and the tree of life. For us to be glorified, our free will, spirit, and body must be presented as a living sacrifice that pleases the Lord. To ask the Lord to show us where our will is not free is the greatest prayer we can pray. Be prepared to see something unexpected.

To be the bride of Christ is to identify with Christ as the bridegroom. The presence of Christ is within you, and you are within Him. It's essential to acknowledge the hidden reality from the tree of life. During the cool part of the day, Adam walked in the garden with God. They were one identity. The illusion of two trees only became relevant when Adam disobeyed God. Only one tree is available for us to eat from. The possibility of sin is always there, but we have a choice. Walking in the garden with God is feasible, or else God wouldn't have called us. Our goal is to surpass our natural deficiencies, heal from our past, and operate from the tree of life. I have firsthand experience with that journey, so I know it's possible. Is perfection part of who I am? Yes. The Lord spoke, "Be perfect just as I am perfect."

According to Satan, we are gods and there's no need to obey the Father. This is why he got kicked out of heaven. I want to make it clear that I'm not implying that we are God, as some people may assume. We are the earthly tabernacle of God's presence and carry the hope of Glory through Christ in us. Not obeying the one true God can turn us into Satan's prideful fallen ways. At the beginning of humankind, the birthright was bestowed upon us by God in our shared garden. Identify with Christ as your hope of Glory by reconnecting through overcoming the fallen nature of self. Remember that you are not God, but you can achieve a state where there is no difference between you and God. Marriage results in the union of one flesh for the bride and groom. Having Christ within us works the same way.

The curse of separation occurred when we gained the ability to differentiate between good and evil. Our truth for the last six thousand years has been nothing but a lie! We could only see what God presented to us through the tree of life with our pure eyes. Is there anyone who wants to see both good and evil?

Count me out!

Prayer

"Lord, show me what is in me that would stop you from being seen upon the earth in a human body."

From that prayer will come answers to see beyond what you can see with your natural fallen nature.

Jesus prayed a prayer: "The time has come, Father, to glorify your son so I can give glory back to you" (John 17:1).

We can't glorify the Lord unless He glorifies Himself in us.

The accomplishments of the human race and the idolisation of humans differ completely from the Glory of the Lord. If ideas are generated in man's mind, they will have death steering the thought or ideas. If accomplishments are done in the spirit, it will have eternal ramifications and bring Glory to the Lord. You can distinguish what originates from human thought and what originates from God's mind if you have crossed that threshold to see with the Lord's eyes, hear with the Lord's ears, and feel with the Lord's heart.

As we approach the realisation of the dream and vision the Lord has given us to carry, we must be cautious it does not become an idol. Remaining outside the vision will result in a contrasting effect from the past. Previously, we had a vision and stood in the vision like a balloon blowing up with us inside that balloon. The illustration is limited to walls and roof. To generate a different outcome from the balloon reality, we must depart from the dream and imagination and allow it to materialise independently from us, but still connected to us. That's timeless space, and it's unrestricted.

Many people have talked about experiencing burnout. People experience burnout due to standing in their power and being wrapped in the old wineskin. God retrieves the old and the new out of the storehouse. But He can't pour new wine into the old wineskin. That expression conveys the idea that God will not abolish everything old, but rather allow it the time to be ushered in to the new. The Lord needs to eliminate all things that have been constructed from man's thoughts to bring His Kingdom, which is His mind, to the earth.

The faithful church has already been stripped of all their baggage so they can carry the mantle of the Kingdom coming to the earth. What we are witnessing now is the stripping of those who had the balloon blown up with them inside. The Lord has popped their balloons (realities) and they are emerging through the bottom of the balloon. That will take some years for them to be washed white and ready for their King's coming. These individuals will be the great multitude coming at the end of the tribulation who have washed their robes. It's their tribulation, and it's their opportunity to be purified. Being loved by the Lord is truly a privilege!

Currently, we find ourselves in the time of sorrow, a period of repentance that will be followed by the tribulation. Tribulation indicates the need to evaluate our understanding, presentation, attachments, possessions, beliefs, labels, etc. That journey required me to overcome for fourteen years. God has set the timing for those who arrived late in this next move. God's move is referred to as the time of Tabernacle. There is a scripture that talks of a vineyard, and some had worked all day in the vineyard and others came later in the day and received the same wage. This passage is applicable here. In the end, we will all be paid the same wages, even though some worked longer. It was invariably about our Lord and His plan, but we made it about ourselves. We are conditioned to be self-focused since infancy. It takes a lot of effort from the Lord to eradicate that thinking and return us to His thinking and His day.

There is a Godly fervency that unites heaven and earth, and there is a desperation that deters the Lord from coming to earth. Let me elaborate! The Lord declared that the fervent prayers of a righteous man avail much. That fervent prayer is holy desperation. The Lord is pushed away by despairs and desperations from the unhealed soul. It has the opposite impact on a situation. This type of desperation generates a gulf between you and the Lord. When we are longing for something to come into existence, we pray, knowing that it is done. That's faith! This faith removes us from the equation and places us in trust, which is everlasting and beyond human comprehension or manipulation.

The human understanding has disregarded the true worshippers of God. But what human understanding was doing was brushing God aside. It won't happen this time around. The Lord's servants will no longer be disregarded, nor will the Lord. This next move of God will have Him stay in humans who have undergone a complete transformation, shining His light. In the former period, religion detained God inside a construction and titled it a church. We, who have been freed from the construction, know that the Spirit of God cannot be controlled or harnessed. Our ego was removed and now we know our identity in the Lord. We have been established in our position as coheirs with the Lord to reign over the earth, with our Lord as the head of all things. God resides with His people and in people in a place on the earth.

Jesus arranged a banquet for us, and we can enjoy it without restrictions. We have encountered all the challenges along the way to be welcomed to this gathering to retrieve our inheritance. Everything that belongs to our Father has now been trusted to us. Christ is our inheritance, and we are His. We will be announced just as Mary was announced and Jesus was announced. This feast is for those who are invited to sit at this table. "Not my will, but your will be done." It's a declaration of God's purpose being fulfilled on earth through

His committed servants and now trusted allies. It's the declaration of Christ's changed body on earth to manifest His Glory and righteousness to all who choose to behold His face. The incarnation of Christ in His elect! If you can declare that you have advanced enough to recognise Christ within you instead of yourself, then you belong to this group of devoted friends of Christ.

After the proclamation is revealed, inclusivity is next. Christ, participating in the earth's events. The end of men's minds, Yay! No longer bypassing the King of King's plans. Just coexisting together as one entity.

Nothing good is being held back. That concept needs to be adopted into our life. Not as a religious text that you know, but His power beyond knowledge. Take another step towards overcoming your limitations. The place I'm talking about goes beyond what you can hope for or imagine.

By peering through the keyhole of our past and entering the doors of our ancestors, we'll discover keys that were left behind with unfinished tasks and missions. A key within a key, another hidden treasure! Only those who dare to seek will ever obtain these keys and bring them into the present now. The keys to the Kingdom of God are these keys. Everything that belongs to Him belongs to us, but are you going to bring it into the earth?

To open new doors with different results, it's important to let go of the keys from the past that haven't produced. If we have a connection or vision that is not fully formed, we must release it and create room for a new manifestation to come from our Lord. I'm not suggesting that the attachment you had isn't a fresh inspiration coming back in a more elevated manner. If it fails to develop into something deeper, it's time to let go permanently. God always provides a new way for you to move forward. Love is the master key for living on a higher platform. Human limitations have prevented us from fully grasping what I am discussing, beyond what I imagined or hoped. The Kingdom of God is symbolised by the tree of life and holds the secrets to a higher existence. It's our Garden of Eden. This garden exists within the life of every person. Some won't fully experience this love because they stop trying and stopped following the King of Glory. The totality is like a feast at a banquet table, offering all the keys to your deepest desires, surpassing your imagination.

In my reality, I caught a glimpse of this flourishing garden. I'm exploring a life that is beyond anything I could have imagined. Merely catching a glimpse won't suffice!

Converting our imagined Garden of Eden into the tangible reality on earth is another undertaking. Start off by dedicating yourself to prayer and fasting. It unlocks heaven's perspective for your eyes and mind. Give up what you can't have, and God will give you what you can't lose.

Our soul connection is linked to Adam, the fallen one who sinned. It's crucial to acknowledge the soul tie and sever your connection. This connection links you to the tree of good and evil. Our soul, spirit, and body are connected to this principality and power. This cut needs to be made in the spirit realm for it to transition into your natural realm.

Wait, but there's more! As coheirs, our mission is to bring His Kingdom to the earth and keep working on it. Challenging self-appointed false authorities within governing bodies. Incorporating every place that obstructs the manifestation of God's plans on earth. Adam defied God and His command, and these authorities are operating under the same fraudulent authority. Human opinions and plans are given priority over God's sovereignty. The earth's fake authority will no longer hold power. God is removing money from the plans of fallen man. When tracing mankind's power, it is connected to money and pride. God commands us to not have two masters, and money has functioned as the other master in this tale. It is finished, are our Lord's famous words! And that's the expression we need to employ.

God will honour His body on earth by vindicating Himself through His transformed disciples. Through prayer, you can embody the glorified Christ. The definition of embody is surrender your body as a living sacrifice, wholly and pleasing to the Lord. It's scriptural. The prayer serves as a bridge between you and God. There is only one spirit, one body, one mind. The separation was our doing, not the Lord's.

The battle between human's dreams and God's dreams is like a great divide. There is only one victor in this battle between fallen man and God. Our Lord's kingdom will be established on earth as in heaven, in a transformed holy people. Humankind's most exceptional attempts need to fail so God can restore His place on earth and dwell with His people. The power that man has had on the earth is over. The timepiece has sounded its designated hour. Wondering how this take back will come about? The Lord always makes a way where there is no way. This division between human actions will be annulled and obliterated from the tree of knowledge of good and evil and the earth. The tie that fallen humanity has had with the serpent is that last bond in that fallen tree. When the manipulative snake whispered into Eve's ear, 'did God really say' is the day we all need to repent of. That's the day humanity pursued their own desires and goals and disregarded God's plans. We have had an unholy alliance to the earth and its plans. This connection with the earth will be restored in holiness once again. Behold, the zeal of God will come and take back what is His. No individual can hinder the unstoppable God from His plans. We have a thousand-year governance on earth with our Lord. And that snake will be hurled into the abyss and confined for the same thousand years.

It's only the voice of our sovereign Lord that deserves our attention. May God rise up in His body to reveal the true power and glory to all humanity. Throughout history, every friend and servant of the Lord has anticipated this moment in time. His glory being lifted up in a renewed population on earth. Taking back what was stolen from the dawn of time. The land of the earth is our inheritance, sworn to us by God through Abraham, Isaac, and Jacob. Our coheir status grants us true power over the land. We have been entrusted with this inheritance by the sovereign Lord.

## CHAPTER 3

## *THE TREE OF LIFE*

It's impossible to glorify a body in a fallen tree. The transformed body should find its place in the tree of life. I am completely overtaken by the Spirit of God. "Behold a man who is fully alive"!

This puts us on a new path never travelled before. Envision dwelling in the tree of life, where love, kindness, gentleness, strength, courage, hope, goodness, laughter, joy, community, mercy, grace, wholesomeness, and other virtues are abundant. The greatest of all is residing with God, as we did in the garden. There's no need for any more battles because the battle has ended. The atmosphere and slip stream are not the same as before. Are you able to feel it? That's what we've inherited! Hope is alive in reality, as promises have been kept. Amazing grace brought us here. We cannot boast since it was a gift from God and not earned by our actions.

No battle indicates the battle is won. We have the opportunity to catch our breath. The door to intimacy with Him is now open. A key to the Kingdom lies in the doorway that leads you into His being instead of His doing. An experience that differs from fighting the good fight and running the race. What would you see if you could look at your own being? It's time to open our eyes and reveal the incredible things He has done within you.

Are you ready?

The Kingdom of God was always within you, but we had to be whole before we could be unveiled as the presence of the Lord on earth. It's your being, not you're doing, that holds the hope of Glory. You are the tree planted by the river, which bears fruit in each season. The leaves never wither, and they prosper in all that they do. That tree the Lord is speaking about is you, and you're in the garden by the river. He is our inheritance, and we are His inheritance. This image reflects both your true self and the Lord as one.

I haven't grasped the Lord's viewpoint on the supernatural yet. The Spirit moves in a similar manner to the wind. You can't see where it comes from, and you can't see where it goes. The supernatural is beyond our comprehension. Supernatural is similar to the wind, it materialises to fulfil its purpose. Begin seeing yourself as God sees you by understanding how He created you. We are fearfully and wonderfully made! Your life's book is a special calling that is written solely for you. Imagine God carefully crafting every individual's life story. He knew us before we were even in our mother's womb. To perceive yourself as the Lord's heir and the representation of Christ is to acknowledge your uniqueness. You're a masterpiece of God's craftmanship on earth. While God is the source of everything, not having a relationship with Him and only seeing Him as a provider is insufficient. What we can give should not be the reason someone loves us. Love delights in your presence.

We experience a new level of connection with God at that point. Our first interaction with Him inspired us to follow in His footsteps. He witnessed our triumph over our sinful nature and our enemies. Your intimacy with Him has grown beyond mere knowledge and salvation. Entering God's essence is what it means to be intimate with Him. The place where you'll experience happiness, pleasure, and laughter. To delight in someone is to find their essence lovely. The goal is to remain with someone who takes delight in your presence. Finding joy in each other's company!

Life's purposes are completed only when we participate in them. God states He will complete the works He started in us. The King's signet ring holds the authority to seal any deals that He has requested you to participate in on earth. The word 'authority' is derived from the word 'author'. God is the author and finisher of our faith. We represent God to the people, as the King's signet ring on earth. You are marked by the Lord for a time such as this. Your future is not determined by your negotiation skills or abilities alone. He is the one who gives good gifts from His treasury and makes the manifestations appear. The plans of our

Lord are fulfilled with those who have sacrificed their lives to follow Him, the King.

The King's signet ring represents the official seal of authority on earth. You are the earthly representative of the Lord's authority. The ring represents covenant, identity, and authority and allows entry to everything that belongs to the King. Overruling evil and reclaiming our birthright for future generations is within our authority. Letting go of old garments is a necessary step to take on your new authority. A woman introduced herself to me by speaking about her illnesses. She proceeded to say that she was starting a new chapter in her life. When starting something new, avoid beginning the conversation with something old. With a desire for a different future, she began by recounting her old story. Jesus left behind His mortal garment in the grave when He resurrected into immortality. Ruth moved on from her widowhood as she entered her new life. Death was left in the grave when Lazarus rose from the dead. What garments are covering your body? Your future clothes are available for you to wear. With new clothes and guidance from the Lord, we move forward.

Request favour and unprecedented access to everything that belongs to the King. Request the Lord's joy and pause to listen to the leaves of the tree applaud as you travel this great path. Pay attention to where the wind is blowing and let it bring you to victory. Your actions will surprise the enemy. Ask for your roots to be watered and for your righteousness to be revealed. Declare that you will enter a new season of life with new nourishment. Ask for the opportunity to hear the stillness of heaven and the stillness of His presence. Ask Him to grant you the ability to hear new sounds. Request that He initiates the new atmospheric change around you. Ask the Lord what action is required for you to move on to the next stage? Pray to the Lord to make your righteousness apparent. The crown of righteousness is upon us; dress and stand in His bestowed righteousness.

Through our Lord Jesus Christ, we can access and release all power on earth. We have access to places that the enemy doesn't. New beginnings signify new domains of influence. The earth is about to experience a new order from the Lord. Unlock the riches in your garden. You have complete access to the Kingdom of God and His throne of grace. His word grants you access to mysteries and revelations. The kingdom's new thinking and Glory can be accessed by all who hold the keys. Understand how God's government functions on earth. In the coming season, God wants to give full authority back to His chosen people. Allow Him to clothe you as you embark on something new. In order to execute this move of God, you will have to use all the keys of the Kingdom. Are you ready?

There is a conflict between God's order and the outdated order structure. The only way to change this discrepancy is through divine intervention. This disorder cannot be changed by anything we do. The Lord of Hosts and His Angel Armies will make it happen.

The earth and everything in it belong to the Lord, and all of humanity is included in this inheritance. The King has sealed us for a time such as this. Order will be restored to the earth by the Lord and His covenant with His Bride (the Church) will be upheld. Our preparation has brought us out of bondage and left us ready for this occasion. Because we are the special possession of the King, the anointing upon us keeps us safe from harm. We are anointed as high priests to stand before

God. And as prophets, we are responsible for offering direction, correction, divine revelations, and leadership to God's people. A holy people!

False accusations become Satan's strategy when you are nearing your destiny. Jesus was falsely accused prior to His crucifixion. The accusation against Joshua was that he lacked the same high priestly clothing as Aaron. Joshua came in his original state, just like the prodigal son, who was embraced by his father. The Lord instructed us to teach, worship, and declare blessings upon the people. Joshua and Jesus both refrained from defending themselves when accused. They chose to have the Father as their defender. As Joshua stepped into leadership and righteousness, the Lord bestowed upon him a new garment. The Lord promises that by walking in His ways and keeping His requirements, you will govern his house and courts. Joshua could access the presence of God as if he were physically present.

Let's talk about why things don't come to earth from heaven. We possess the keys to both heaven and earth. Jesus obtained the keys and then gave them to us. A common phrase that I've heard over the years is: "I'm waiting on God." That saying is delivered with a gentle voice, with no aspiration to be God's seal of authority on earth. We can move God's hand by seeking divine insight into the cause of delays. I came to the realisation that I wasn't showing proper respect for time or space. I desired things to occur now, in my time and space. Beyond our temporal realm, the Lord reigns over our space and time and all other spaces and times. These elements must be respected in order for God's supernatural timing to be revealed. Hand over your time and space to the Lord and see how things begin to shift. Or drop your clichés and become the Lord's signet ring seal of authority upon the earth.

Identifying who the Lord has designed you to be is crucial to securing your inherent future. The creation of humans is both magnificent and fearful, but our comprehension of ourselves is hindered by life constraints and circumstances. We've been living our life story, but another parallel love story has been tracking us all along. We've been unable to handle the higher reality, as our minds were not yet ready to accept it. It's not until you come to the end of the old story that the entry point to the new dimension will be revealed. This new life will take us to a level beyond our ordinary existence and make it a life worth living. God brings the old out with the new. Allow your mind to receive what was previously invisible for you to see. Pray to the Lord to show you more of Himself through His creative perspective and appreciate the beauty of His love in this new way. It's up to you to decide if you want to access this dimension or stay in the ordinary humdrum of life.

A challenging mix of good and evil has made up life thus far. Love has had the ability to show us a way to escape the ordinary mundane if we are willing to ask and take up the offer. Life's conversations ensnare us in the tree of morality like a suffocating snake, manipulating our existence and thoughts. We have been emotionally invested in the narrative because this is the only form of love that we have known. Follow the path beyond the dead tree and into the tree of life, where new beginnings and new stories await. A place that we cannot fully grasp with our minds because we haven't got there yet. New understandings of love will emerge all around us as we venture to this higher way. The surrounding atmosphere will overflow with love, and you will be dancing to its music.

Observing humanity through the eyes as the Lord God is a repentance like I've never experienced before. The Lord sees humanity with a heart full of love. He fails to perceive our sins and shortfalls. His eyes behold those who He created perfectly. It's imperative that we see through those eyes. To see something below - that is to see with the eyes of the fallen man through the tree of good and evil. The sins of mankind are only an illusion that misleads us into believing they are real. There's nothing genuine in that fallen tree except repentance.

To enter the tree of life, one must sense the suffering of being unloved by fallen man. If you don't feel remorse, you're not coming out of the fallen tree. Our realisation of humanity's absence of affection towards us compels us to seek the Lord's guidance in transitioning us into a new realm of life and love beyond the fallen tree. As women, we face another subconscious challenge created by men. Men hold a fear and disrespect of women at a deep, unconscious level. The fear in man developed when woman led him out of God's Garden. It is essential that this division ends for men and women to coexist in unity. This division can only be eliminated by the love of God. The woman's prayers have the power to cause transformation from the Lord. The praying is finished! Men, be careful. You might find yourself liking us sooner than you realise. The Lord wants us to dwell together in harmony and unity. It's necessary for men to forgive women. The old Adam's bloodline was terminated by Jesus' death on the tree. But to access the Tree of Life and bring about change, we must acknowledge the existence of Adam's seed within our subconscious and repent.

Some time ago, I began a journey to conquer my sinful nature. I spent twelve years alone, sleeping next to the rivers in Australia. Shaking with cold on a particular night, the Lord's voice from within spoke to me, asking if I was cold? "Yes, Lord, I said!" He described this is how men felt after being banished from the garden. He asked me to repent on behalf of all women all the way back to Eve. I made it a point to explain and apologise to any men I interacted with over the next few days. Initially, they seemed angry, but after I took responsibility for what we, as women, had done, they accepted my apology and moved on. Repentance is a pathway in two directions. It is necessary for both men and women to repent.

CHAPTER 4

## *TRUE AUTHORITY AND LOVE*

To truly live in God's authority, we must take another step to uncovering what prevents us from reaching our garden and promised land. A friend of mine said that since women led men out of the garden, women will lead them back in. This idea resonates with me because I believe that men and women coexisting peacefully can attract the Lord's blessing and build His Kingdom on earth. How good and pleasant it is when brothers live in harmony. The term 'brothers' can refer to both men and women.

The only way to get to this wonderful garden is by revisiting the tree of good and evil to ascertain where we are falling short of His Glory. Based on my assessment, it seems that few individuals are living up to their full potential with true authority. The fallen tree has tainted us. Overcoming false authority is essential for the arrival of His Kingdom onto the earth. This false authority lives in both men and women. It's widespread for people to walk around with a fake sense of authority. They possess the knack of lowering their voice and delivering impactful words. They could be using titles to boost their self-importance. This does not reflect true authority.

To follow the path of the Lord, the authority comes from heaven, not from titles, voices, or words. A genuine authority figure doesn't mislead others into believing there's hope. False hope originates from the dead tree! False authority rejected both their own inheritance and the Lord's inheritance. Due to the fallen tree reality, most of us have either surrendered or do not hold our rightful authority. This has short changed us of our birthright!

Our God is amazing and has the power to restore all that has been lost or seems lost. The responsibility of reclaiming our inheritance and authority in the Lord lies with us as we journey through our own fallen nature. We all have been guilty of submitting to false authority at some time. Everyone is guilty of giving false hope to someone. We, as the Lord's people, have the responsibility to treat each other with the same respect and honour that the Lord embodies. Walking there means we're walking in the tree of life. The highest commandment is to love one another!

The occurrence happening now on earth will bring about the fulfillment of God's original plan for man and woman. By enabling both men and women to experience freedom from trauma, they can become the person God intended them to be. Reflecting His image and glory here on earth as it is in heaven.

I asked the Lord when we first met why there were so many church buildings with different names. I heard His voice asking me to turn on the radio. It was a service in the Catholic faith. The government was prayed for at the end of the service. The Lord spoke again and said that people are interceding for the government, making music, and doing mission work and many other tasks that people can't see. He stated that upon His return for His bride, He will take one person from this place and another from that place. The Lord made it clear He was only interested in the heart of man, not their works. I understood that it's not my responsibility to worry about how people do things, it's up to the Lord. Every individual has their own unique expression because we are all wonderfully different. As the body of Christ, we all have unique roles to play. I may not be able to build or repair things, but I excel at bringing people together. Over time, I've observed the attempts of organised denominations to unite, but they were unsuccessful due to our strong attachment to their cultural expressions. Just as we are currently seeing with Aboriginals holding tight to their culture, as are the settlers holding on to their culture. As friends and representatives of Christ, it's important to look beyond our cultural differences. The Lord transcends culture! He represents freedom to be our true selves, without the constraints of culture, titles, knowledge, or words. This creates unity. Unity commands the blessings of the Lord. Loving and accepting each other is the key to bringing heaven to earth.

The Lord removed me from society, and with it went my titles, money, culture, and possessions. It felt like stepping down from my self-elevated throne and discarding my robes. As time progressed so did my existence into nothingness. I was brought to my knees! From this place, I saw a keyhole directly in front of me. Behind the keyhole was a city which was His Kingdom.

In the old days, camels would kneel and remove their packs to enter the city gates. The gates had the shape of keyholes. My experience felt the same as the camel's experience. Removing all things that we find attractive and heavy is necessary to enter His Kingdom. Come as you were created, not with what you can give or carry.

Acceptance of one another in our present situation is part of the Lord's love. I took a woman on a camping trip with the intention of teaching her how to camp. She mentioned her friend's tragic passing during that period. He was identified as gay! According to her, his only desire was to return to God, but the lifestyle's shame prevented him from facing God. He died with horror on his face. We, as God's people, must understand that God still loves and is connected to those who have taken a different turn in their lifestyle. It's not our place to condemn them by forcing scriptures on them. They are aware of being in sin. Regrettably, the religious culture was unable to cope with these people, resulting in either rejection or a shift in their beliefs to the point where they no longer reflected the House of the Lord.

I provided shelter to two sisters who were homeless out on the street. The father of the girls used to invite his friends over to get drunk and locked his daughters in a room with a bag of marijuana. The men came for the girls after they were fully intoxicated with grog. I came into the picture at that point. Today, one of these girls has become a lesbian and has tattoos all over her body. I brought them to a church, but the church didn't take care of her and her sister, so they left and became who they are today. Every time she calls me, she begins the conversation the same way. "I don't know what would've happened to us girls if you hadn't come along." When life becomes overwhelming for the girls, they turn to me after thirty and more years. Christ never left them, but they find Christ in me. Her lesbianism is a result of the abuse she faced at the hands of those men. We have the ability to alleviate the suffering of those individuals. It's time to view them as human beings and not the disgrace of the sin. We have left them in their sins because many rejected them as people. To be considered a body of Christ, every walk of life must be included. The statements I make have certain conditions attached. I think that if someone is committing a sin, they should be excluded from the community walls until they get it under control. The prohibition includes sorcery, sexual immorality, drugs, and drunkenness etc. It's just different manifestations of sin. What's the reason for tolerating one but not the other?

Through two gay men, I found my way to the Lord. Years ago, not long after, my inflatable world fell for the first time. I traded in my new Pulsar Q, car for a long wheelbase troop carrier and headed to the desert. My children still have nightmares about a song I played during that long trip. The song, For Non-Blondes, 'Trying to get up that great big hill '. That's where I was at! My goal was to fulfil the brief that the world presented to me. Husband, house, family and business was that brief. I lost it all in an instant, but at least I still had my children.

My career began as a photographer for models and actors, but I eventually transitioned into running my own acting agency. All the way on the desert trip, my head was thinking about my next move. My lifestyle before the crash included ninety-six light bulbs illuminating my home, along with a full staff, maids, and cooks who catered to my every need. Additionally, all my clothes were tailor made because I worked with models and actors. However, I was unaware of who the Lord God was. The concepts of church, Sunday school, God, and Jesus were completely foreign to me. The way I would describe myself in the past is different from how I would describe myself today. During my desert journey, I arrived at Ayers Rock, now commonly called Uluru. I got out of my 4XWD and saw a dingo. I grabbed my camera off the seat, and without setting exposures, I took the photo. Without meaning to, the dingo shot triple exposed. After returning to Sydney to get myself back on track, I developed the film. This picture featured a dingo with a triple exposure, giving the impression of a ghostly dingo on top of Ayers Rock. Therefore, the name given to the shot was 'Ghost Dingo'. This photo led me to my next business venture, animal photography.

Within weeks, I established a mobile studio in the dog field and began creating portfolios for breeders. Little did I know a charming man was watching me. He started by stating that he had authored fourteen books and owned two magazines. He put his card on my desk in my studio. After several weeks of meeting him in the dog fields, he paid me a visit at my house. He suggested that I bring my daughters and myself and live at his beach house. He also suggested that I photograph his magazines and books, and in return, he would lend me a hand in launching my new business. What appeared to be a good offer turned into a nightmare very soon.

Once I arrived, his gay friend appeared, and to this day, he remains the most poisonous person I've ever met. The entire scheme to bring me to his house was a set up. Being gay was not considered cool 30 years ago. To avoid being seen as gay by his publishers, he brought a woman and two children into his life.

His homosexual buddy was looking to harm me by leaving his AIDS-infected needles around. Instead of a room in the house, I ended up with a mattress on the garage floor next to the biggest dope plant owned by Mr. Hydroponics, the magazine owner. Losing my identity as a wife, business owner, and possessions made me believe that I had hit rock bottom. This reached a whole new level. I felt like I was on the edge of a cliff, holding onto a ladder with just my little finger. Or walking on a tightrope, and it seemed like death was waiting for me. Suddenly, my first prayer came to me! My words were: if there is a God, get me out of here! He not only got me out of there, but He also transformed me into his very special possession. I've witnessed the gay lifestyle from within and it's the most terrible thing I've ever seen. As the Lord transformed me to see things from His perspective, we must find a way to help those who wish to leave that lifestyle and return to their rightful place in His Kingdom. Failing to love our neighbour as ourselves means we haven't fulfilled the great commission.

We see through the glass dimly. I had lunch with a man who firmly believed his decisions were good decisions. Everyone makes decisions, or else we wouldn't be able to move forward. Our decisions can't be good if we're seeing through a dim glass! Our Lord's perspective is the only way to make decisions. He will always reveal the way forward if you seek and wait for Him. Unfortunately, people are not abiding in the Lord's way. Our society has been shaped by the decisions of men and women influenced by the fallen nature and the tree of good and evil. It's been a thirty-year journey for me to get over my fallen nature and to see things from the Lord's perspective. Have I reached my destination yet? Not at this moment, otherwise I would be in the promise. The path to liberating oneself from yourself is a step-by-step process. Line upon line, precept upon precept.

In the thirty years since I came to know the Lord, my perspective on things has shifted. I don't have the same judgement upon people or situations as before. The Lord has granted me the gift of great discernment. The Lord says not to judge anything before the appointed time. That isn't what 99.9% of people are doing. Everyone has an opinion on the information they're being fed about the government, cultures, churches, medical field, and media. I haven't had a TV in any of my living spaces for more than two decades. I'm cut off from radio, news feeds, Facebook, and social media platforms. I reside on 700 acres, far from the hustle and bustle of civilization. In order to become holy and rid oneself of the world's narrative, I believe you must spend some time alone with the Lord only. As my time is almost over, I aim to establish a holy place with the Spirit of God at the heart of a community. It will go beyond names and culture, and it will include all walks of life. It will mirror the Lord's outlook, not mankind's thinking. The earth will be blessed with the presence of God's Spirit living among men and women in this community. Decisions will be made by the Lord and not by the fallen human minds. I sacrificed my fallen nature to get here. To lay down your bodies as a living sacrifice was the accurate terminology used by our Lord.

In writing four books, I've tackled the challenge of overcoming my inherent sinful nature. This book will transport me back to the garden of God within me. It's not just me who can go. I have to keep the door open in faith for others to follow. Otherwise, I'll be living in my garden without anyone to share it with. The Lord God commanded us to go and multiply, but we did so in the fallen tree rather than in the garden of God. Imagine a place where the multiplication of people is being restored to its proper place in the garden.

Walking with God during the cool part of the day! There's no greater thought that comes to mind. My desire aligns with the Lord's - for us to love one another. It's time to start moving towards our destiny as a people who love the Lord God with all our heart. Today is the day we've been waiting for. Just do it!

For as long as mankind has been in the fallen tree, the mind of man has been under the spell of false authority. If you are, you're submitting to witchcraft. Witchcraft is present in many cultures, geographies, and anything that goes beyond our Lord's intentions. You are the elected ones of God. Why do you allow others to dictate your way forward? Assert your authority and resist the enemy. Someone told me, a man discovered a python snake in his garden. This man was a representation of land, they added. The serpent snake is a dream time story for the Aboriginals, whereas the Bible talks about a serpent that tricked a woman at the forbidden tree. The Lord caused enmity between humanity and the woman. That enmity is between the serpent and humanity. I step on its head and crush it if I see that serpent anywhere near me. In my language, we call the serpent Satan. In the Aboriginal language, it is recognised as the rainbow serpent, which created the beginnings of human existence. Their culture perceives this serpent as living in the waters and moving like a dragon.

The Bible interprets Leviathan spirit as a sea monster with many heads. The crossover parallels the biblical account, with the exception that we acknowledge the Father of heaven and earth as the Creator from the beginning. The deceiver was the snake. The Aboriginals have developed the practice of seeking permission before entering a sacred site, where the serpent may be present. If the snake we're discussing is the same one mentioned in the Bible, then submitting to the false authority that Satan no longer holds would be the case here. Jesus Christ rectified this on the cross. All things are restored and put right so we can enter our garden promised land with the Lord. Satan is banned. Fear is not allowed in the garden. The spirit realm, let alone this serpent, is a mystery to most people. 'My people perish from lack of knowledge'. I have never seen a truer saying from the Lord. The Lord caused the death of thousands during the desert crossing due to their failure to grasp His ultimate plan. Other idols were worshiped by them before the Lord.

The fight for land is relevant now because the Lord requires His land back. We believe the fight is between Aboriginals and white settlers. No, it is greater than that. The Lord desires to live on earth as in heaven. But if we continue to hold the view that this land is ours, reconsider. Control of the land slipped away from the true rulers and was taken over by the serpent snake. We were caretakers of our land and that got lost back at the garden of God six thousand years ago and it carries into today. But the Lord restored that loss at the cross. It's our responsibility as believers in the Lord to reclaim His land from those with false power. Take back what was stolen! This taking back begins and ends in the soul of mankind. The Lord is emphasising a point here. It's not the land of the Aboriginals or the white settlers, but rather the land of the Lord God who will use the land as He desires. The Lord God is sovereign over the land and also you! Both parties are out of line with the Lord's vision for this earth. They view things through their dim glass that is coloured by their culture. The fight is not in the natural world, it's in the spirit realm. And that spirit lives in you. We do not fight against flesh and blood, but against principalities and powers. Principalities and powers live in the atmosphere in you, and you project it into the earth. Witchcraft, words of claiming this is my land because I got here first or I have the piece of paper saying I can be here, it's all rubbish in the Lord's eyes.

God granted people the land to accomplish His plan on earth. Failing to fulfil the Lord's plan will lead us to be considered as the wicked servant who buried his talent in the ground and faced punishment from the Lord. Imagine having a plot of land but neglecting the Lord's vision and allowing the serpent to take control. Correction is essential, otherwise the Lord will take it back Himself.

They hung the Lord on the dead tree, which represents the tree of good and evil. It was then that Satan lost his dominance over the earth and all its inhabitants. That's the point where everything was restored. That's when His Kingdom was brought to earth. Our limited perspective fails to fully communicate the richness of this act. We understand God sent His Son to make a path for everyone to return to the Father of life. We comprehend that Jesus' sinless nature cancelled death. Overcoming our sinful nature, all the way back to the first Adam, is made possible by this act. What other insights can we get from this?

Let's Explore!

Jesus granted forgiveness to all, surrendered His spirit to the Father, and His body breathed its last. After that, He was laid in the tomb. He rose from the tomb after three days and appeared in many places for forty days.

What was He showing us?

I delved into the significance of glorified bodies on earth in my previous book. My friend and I have a prophecy about glorified bodies walking on earth. The Lord comes again for His Bride with no spot or blemish. The Lord separated me from the rest of the world and told me I was never to drink alcohol again. He removed me from social groups because He didn't want me to be confined to a label. He stripped me of my honours or titles because that inflated my sense of self-importance. God removed my successes because they made me feel too boastful. The Lord took away my belongings and fancy, expensive clothes because I valued them. In other words, He removed from me everything the world would acknowledge as valuable. He set me apart for Himself and called me His special possession. Why would God go that far? To complete the restoration and restore His kingdom to the earth.

What is the resurrection? Christ is alive here on earth in human form once again. The Holy Spirit, our Comforter, was given to us by Jesus to indwell our beings. As we conquer our sinful nature, we invite Jesus Christ to fill the void that sin once occupied in our lives. This extended sequence of events ultimately results in you becoming Christlike, with your thoughts and actions aligned with His. You transform into His likeness, it's in accordance with scripture. It's no longer I who lives, it's Christ who lives in me.

The Lord talks about how His righteousness and Glory will be seen through us. We bear His mind and spirit, whilst exhibiting His righteousness and Glory to the outer world. What is the appearance? The manifestation of Christ on earth, as in heavenly bodies on earth. Satan was expelled because he believed he was God, and if we do the same, we will face the same destiny. The Lord made sure that this scenario wouldn't happen by helping us move past our prideful fallen nature. The bride has been prepared by Him, without spot or blemish. The body is in the process of being glorified. The groom (Christ) will glorify His bride when He comes in a twinkling of an eye. This is a phenomenon that surpasses the arrival of the Holy Spirit.

The stillness of the Spirit is not evidence that the Lord is not active. What the Lord has penned in the manuscripts is brought to life every day. The Spirit's perpetual movements are like that of the wind or air, crossing lands to reach His people. To see beyond oneself and into another's eyes is akin to seeing into the eyes of the Lord. In anticipated love, we wait for the occasion the promise is fulfilled. The foundation of things hoped for is our resting place as the day unfolds, as a gift from our God.

It's not good for man to be alone, as our Lord once said. Humanity's solitary existence will be replaced by a sense of community as we return to the Tree of Life once more. The collapse of mankind has led to our temporal lives being occupied with insignificant tasks, conversations, and issues. We value these tasks because Christ's mysteries are beyond our immediate understanding, causing us to retreat into what we know. Those who have a deep love for the Lord will experience unimaginable things and answer His call. Our feet will tread into something beyond the ordinary fallen world, something greater than we ever hoped for. Each day produces His extraordinary imagination. It's up to us if we want to perceive each day as mundane or appreciate His unparalleled creativity, showing us the way home. A moment with God is worth more than any ordinary moment. When we move towards the unknown, we need to let go of our familiar lifestyle and ways. Sadly, we've become accustomed to the life given to us by a fallen humanity. Letting go of the conversation and perception of the world is releasing oneself from the restrictions of a regimented lifestyle. Our aim is to discover what lies beyond our current sight as we seek the prize and goal set by the Lord. "We ask, Lord, open our eyes and reveal to us the unseen and unheard things." Expect the unexpected!

As we seek to be holy like the Father, our love on earth has progressed to a higher level. It's this same love that will lead us to uncharted territories beyond our imagination. The love I'm referring to depends on breaking free from the daily routine, material possessions, capabilities, knowledge, concerns, and communication of the world. Love made earth its training arena. Living on earth seems like being part of a movie called 'The Truman Show' with Jim Carey. He came into the world in a fictitious town, with a fictional family and make-believe job. Over time, he became aware of the flaws in the routine he lived in. He was discouraged from exploring outside the town due to the fear instilled in him by the movie people. As he began to put the pieces together, he overcame his fear of water and crossed an ocean to get to the back of the movie set. He made his way up the stairs, bowed to the audience, and said, "Good afternoon, good evening, and good night," as a parting message in case he didn't meet them again. He proceeded to open the door of the movie set and exit into his newfound freedom.

Routines, knowledge, and possessions are all part of life on earth. If I was Satan, I'd keep individuals in the routine of life to avoid them seeking an exit from the world. You have heard the saying, 'stop the world; I want to get off!' Triumphing over our sinful self is the way to access those keys to that prison cell of routine and cancelling our debt of belong to this world. Looking beyond the world to the supreme love in our Father's eyes is necessary to receive the love we're longing for. This world will never care for us as our Father in heaven cares. To fulfil the call, we must learn to love the simple things in life and release ourselves from the world's distractions. The Lord talks about a glorified body walking here on earth. His righteousness will be visible, and His glory will be upon those who have overcome. What I'm discussing here is beyond what we have seen or heard. To be on earth as this glorified body will free us from the ordinary routines. It will cause heaven to come to earth in a human physical body. "We ask you, Lord, to glorify us with your Glory, just as we were glorified with you before time began."

Seek the Lord's face and everything will be added. It is possible for the earth to be viewed as an idol in the eyes of the Lord. The world's worries can also have that effect. The pursuit of work and toil in the world can distract us from seeking the Lord's face or finding the keys to the prisons that encase us in our environments. People live their lives without seeking the Lord's face. There are those who know scriptures better than I do. There are individuals who think that serving the Lord is a guarantee to enter heaven. Others focus on acquiring knowledge. Eliminate all distractions and focus on seeking His face. Each of us has fallen short of His Glory. Every morning, the sun's Glory rises, reminding us to aim higher. As the sun rises, we take a moment to express gratitude for the day ahead. The dawning of the sun is signalling us to, 'lift up our heads O you gate, so the King of Glory can come in'. To witness what we haven't seen, we need to elevate our heads from the tasks and cares to look into His face.

The mind's illusions have determined an already-established existence on earth. It is shaped by our wants, needs, and ambitions, as well as our hereditary bloodlines. To create something different will take a people who see with the Lord's eyes and hear with the Lord's ears. Year after year, the land becomes more exhausted, and the soil is contaminated. The people are unwilling to change their ways despite being sick from its poisons sprayed on their food and the poisons injected in their land. They persist in their established routines with a false hope of recovery. What can be done to break their pattern of self-annihilation? Illnesses force them to stop and prevent them from following their routines. That halts their physical being, but how can their mindset be transformed into a new healthy lifestyle? Only God can accomplish that! Our physical composition is derived from the soil of the land. Your body reflects the atmosphere surrounding you. The Lord brings you into a place with an intention of understanding your surroundings and conquer your environment, which is connected to your body. People often sit in their own demise, failing to understand God's message every day. Deception can come in smokescreens and curses, while toiling the land can be a never-ending curse for some. What environmental elements must be observed to reach a state of holiness in your area of abode?

Observing humanity's current state instils hope for the revealing of the King and His Kingdom. This is our only remaining hope! Many have tried, and many have failed to restore this broken world. Throughout generations, the return of the Lord has been eagerly awaited. People become weary of waiting and have fallen asleep. Others wait in anticipation of His return. They've kept oil in their lamps in the hope of His return. Our dreams of the revealing King's return are restored and reignited when we see the possibilities on our path ahead. Today is the day we have waited for 'the King's unveiling'. Stir up your heart once more if you can't see this.

Every day presents us with chances to love others. Every day is a chance to break free from the toxins sprayed by humanity into our minds and bodies. The official explanation is that it will help us grow, but in reality, it's a tactic to control humans and keep us from broadening our horizons. The tree planted by the river is a representation of us, and we hold the power to grow into the Tree of Life. Eliminate toxins in your mind and bloodstream by renewing your mind with the Lord's word. Through the saints' prayers, may your body and blood be healed. Your body's soil is equivalent to the land and environment where you live and occupy. Yesterday, I made room for the King to magnify Himself through my body - a sacred land that belongs to Him - by conquering the toxic atmosphere that surrounded me. My internal person has been reached with glorification through different levels of overcoming. The recovery of my mind and bloodline is a success, but my soil remains in need of restoration. My focus now is solely on Christ's dedication to bringing Glory to Himself through a human form. Having hope of His coming makes me confident that I'm in a good place to receive. Our hearts cry out for the coming of Our Lord Jesus Christ.

"I had a dream," as Martin Luther King once said. In this dream, I saw the Holy Spirit touch many diverse people with His spirit. It was an outpouring of His spirit. I was in the room and when I laid hands on cancer patients; the cancer disappeared. When I spoke to people, their minds were freed. It was beyond anything that I'd seen in my walk with the Lord. It was a fresh outpouring of the Spirit of God, and it didn't go away; it stayed, and so did the people. The only way out of this mess that mankind has created is by His spirit. The free will of humanity has reached its peak of iniquity. People want to get out of the mind structure of this mess. The Lord comes when the cries of our heart reach His throne.

I then saw it was up to me to release what had been established inside of me. His righteousness, His love, His Hope, His Faith, and His Glory. All the power of the Spirit was already in me and had been critiqued over the years to become the fullness of Him who lives in me. The Hope of Glory!

The one who has come and will come again goes beyond human suffering, the curse of the land, and our free will. The KING revealed as human once again walking on earth is the second coming. Knowing about His coming is not enough to receive glorification; one must also overcome their fallen nature to receive. The upcoming event will unveil the 144,000 virgins of the heart spoken of in the Lord's scripture. Acknowledging the reality we are living and letting it go is necessary for Christ's transformation to come into His desired human state. We are witnessing a happening beyond our reality and imagination. Purging ourselves of any life regrets or regrets imposed on us is necessary. Through this process, purity can manifest flawlessly in the human body.

The exclusive obstruction to receiving the King's fullness is ourselves. Satan was at the scene in the garden of God, and Eve fell victim to his deception by believing the lie. Satan resides within all our souls because we are part of the human race. And God states we all fell short of His glory and were deceived. The process of removing Satan from the human soul has been challenging, but the results are worth it. Give this some thought! Without recognising Satan as an illusion, we cannot perceive the true reality of heaven on earth. If your earth is contaminated with illusions of mankind's fall and destruction, you won't perceive heaven on earth. The concept of the fall and destruction is a product of Satan's manipulation, tricking your mind into perceiving their existence as reality. If people put an end to looking at the world's destruction, our eyes would only see heaven on earth.

The heavens declare His Glory! Being subject to the earth's gravity leads to the bending of light and the slowing down of time. When light penetrates and illuminates the soul, we are slowly revealing heaven on earth. As humans, we are the embodiment of heaven's reflection and image on earth, and we are part of God's garden on earth. The light of God bends our mind (soul) to enter and establish heaven on earth. There is a similarity to a black hole in space where gravity is incredibly powerful, preventing light from escaping once it entered. This light is God dwelling with people and in people. The light inside us remains on earth, only growing brighter as it breaks free from the outer form. Compared to the glorified body Christ had after His resurrection, our light is minimal. What part of us holds the key to breaking free from the constraints of our mortal bodies? Or is the breaking in His hands so we can't boast? Christ's presence within us and our existence within Him leads to the second coming, which happens when the Son aligns with the earth, similar to an eclipse. This alignment becomes the completion of the process of overcoming our fallen nature. This completion will bring about the second coming and glorification on earth, where people reflect His glory in His entirety. God calls many, but not all will reveal His glory in human form. The fullness that exists within each person has been taken over by the distractions of the world or works. I've noticed a mindset in the Christian community that believes being born again and saved is sufficient for the upcoming transformation. That thought is deceptive and falls short of His Glory. Many in that community will experience disappointment and anger, leading to the great falling away. The elect is not exempt from being deceived.

Our inheritance is the same as the King's inheritance, resuming His rightful position in a victorious individual. Behold, a man fully alive!

When Jesus rose from the grave, angels rolled the rock away from in front of the tomb. That tomb was a visual representation of mankind's deceased body. During Jesus' time in the tomb, a happening occurred, which can't be explained because its supernatural. This happening transformed His dead body to a glorified body. And that glorified body walked the earth. Jesus shows us the way all the way. He doesn't leave us in the grave or on the cross. Upon His resurrection, many others came out of their graves as well. The scriptures suggest that saints who conquered their sinful nature can walk the earth with Him. We are on the brink of this supernatural happening again. When we let go of everything, we open ourselves up to a new form of existence. Our body's molecules are magnetically attracted to Christ's body's molecules, representing the awaited supernatural transformation.

When the Lord's Glory is unleashed, it will touch everyone, regardless of their status. Only those who have reached the end of themselves will experience the full Glory. As Glory descends, it fills the depths of the soul, inspiring some to begin their journey and propelling others forward in theirs. Newcomers will be empowered to match the efforts of seasoned workers for Christ through a spiritual quickening. The newcomers will receive equal wages as those who have faithfully served Christ for a long time.

The scripture about having oil in your lamp is widely known. The purpose of this oil is to attract the bridegroom to His ready bride. The living Glory of Him resides in you as oil. Are people actually ready or is it just a statement of knowing a scripture? You're not ready if your mind is not Christ's mind. If you're still burdened by hurts, regrets, and unforgiveness, you're not prepared. If you haven't overcome all obstacles, you're not ready. The confession of a scripture is not what Christ is looking for. We need to achieve total victory over life's struggles. The Lord's care extends to what's happening in the world, relieving us of our worries in the world. I don't partake in spreading slander or gossip because that's not the God I'm familiar with. The love of the King should determine the order of possession and ownership. We are entrusted with being stewards of the Lord's possessions. However, those possessions should not be turned into idols.

Without the Lord God as your primary love, you won't be ready for the transformation of the King and His prepared bride. Idol talk plays a role in overcoming and judging others. In many ways, titles and culture have become idols. Going for the goal and running the race is how we prepare for the King's return so He can exalt His bride. Pray to the Lord for insight into your areas of unpreparedness. The oil in the lamp is a revelation of you being fully alive and radiating His light. You are the divine lamp.

Throughout history, we have witnessed the Lord's forgiving nature. People are given authority or a title by Him, and they tend to use it for their own advantage. Humans in positions of stewardship are susceptible to deception if they haven't conquered their fallen nature. The Lord tells us to put all spirits to the test! While we may be born again, knowledgeable in scriptures, and have a ministry, misusing our appointed platform for personal gain won't be pleasing to the Lord.

I recently came across a story from a ministry that helps the homeless. In the story, the man mentioned his political views and labelled anyone who disagreed as heartless. He falsely claimed that dreams didn't come true. This isn't a symbol of our Lord God! The minister used what he received from the Lord to promote his own political agenda. It's not a good reflection of our Lord God for others to witness. It must grieve the Lord to witness His servants using their position for self-interest.

Our own soul is a place where the devil must be constantly monitored. He roams around in that place because your soul reflects your inner wounds into the outside world. The things you dislike in your world are where your opportunities for growth lie. Request the Lord's help in conquering the mental battlefield and experience freedom of thought. The more you value freedom of thought, the more determined you become to achieve your dreams. In the front cover of my first book, 'How I Overcame My Own Life,' I have a saying that I write. 'To change your world, you change your mind.' With new thoughts comes new freedom, with new freedoms comes true happiness.

I got happy because I changed my mind. Imagine, a happy woman!

Outside our realm of consciousness! Our minds have limited us to a daily routine and a prescribed way of thinking. The vision the Lord has given us often takes a backseat to our daily to-do list. The Lord's plans may be overshadowed by the distractions of today's battle. We must prioritise our lives to become who the Lord intended us to be. While some people prioritise pleasure, others prioritise work in order to enjoy holidays and acquire material things. While I have no issue with work, it concerns me when people prioritise pleasures over the Lord's business. In my eyes, they have not yet merged themselves completely with the Lord. There is no separation from the love of God.

A few thoughts about consciousness have crossed my mind. The kingdom of God is within us, yet we still lack what has been promised. Why? The shackles of mental limitations hold us back! God has bestowed upon us gifts that we have not yet uncovered, making us whole. The act of transporting through walls, as Jesus did and raising people from the dead, just to mention a couple of examples. Our potential remains unfulfilled as our conscious mind confines us within the boundaries of our daily world. To see beyond the familiar, we must extend our tent pegs and borders. Let our eyes be opened to understand the truth, for it will bring us freedom. The Lord's infinity makes us infinite. There are no limitations because we are made in His image. Do we prioritise ourselves or the Lord in each day? Each believer should ask themselves daily if they are sacrificing their life wholly and pleasingly to the Lord. Every day, His Grace and Mercies are new, making our requests fresh every morning. Take a careful look at your life to determine your limitations and priorities.

Division in our society comes by categorising people into groups. The Lord sees individuals, not groups. His intention is to come for the heart of man, not their group. There are many labels people use, such as elites, gays, lefts, rights, saved, unsaved, and the list goes on. The Lord only sees the person, not their group name. Not aligning your thoughts with the Lord can have consequences. The desire of God is for no one to be lost, and He uses the Holy Spirit, who is within us, to reach people. To categorise someone is to create a division. We shouldn't judge anyone before the appointed time since the end has not come.

I had an incident with a wonderful lady who is worth her weight in gold. Her mind was tricked into thinking she had to take responsibility for everyone around her. However, she could not recognise her own value and worth. Our true value can remain hidden when affirmation is absent in our lives. We categorise ourselves into our own groups: 'just you' or 'just me'. In God's eyes, we are valuable, worthy, and uniquely created. If we can't see ourselves as the Lord does, we haven't fully embraced His Glory for our entrusted life. Our existence is purposeful and wonderfully designed for a plan on earth. Break out of the confines of your self-categorisation. This is just one constraint on your mind. Embrace your true identity. Shine that bright light!

I stood in line and took part in voting for the first time. The reason behind my lack of voting was my lack of understanding of the system at eighteen; I told myself I would vote once I understood it. At the age of sixty-five, I realised that my mind was no longer my own; it belongs to Christ, and the transformation had been completed. This understanding allowed me to have a vote. Next time, I'll remember to bring a roll of gaffer tape for my mouth! I am confident in my identity in Him, which enables me to speak the truth without hesitation. Whether they want to hear the truth, you are the difference people need. Take a stand for what is right and good and become the difference. Rise above the self-imposed categories you're in. Cross the finish line with flying colours.

If the government rests on His shoulders, then it rests on ours. We are the physical manifestation of Christ's body on earth.

## CHAPTER 5

## *NO WALLS*

How would you define the body of Christ? I was under the impression that everyone who identified as a Christian was the body of Christ. The entire large group, with no additional individuals. I was specifically instructed by God to only use my birth name, not group names or titles, in my walk with Him. I transformed into an unknown entity, wholeheartedly pursuing Christ. Like a treasure hunter, I seek God with unwavering devotion, listening to His voice unveil unknown mysteries. I believe in Christ in a way that surpasses just identifying as Christian. I no longer see the body of Christ as exclusive to Christians. Curious about how God described His body, I sought His perspective, and here's what I found.

Offer your body as a living sacrifice, wholly and pleasing to the Lord. Without embodying this scripture, it remains mere words. As we have overcome our minds, we have been transformed. And His Word is now embedded in our hearts. Our past has been healed and our enemies have been forgiven. With love as our lens, we judge righteously through our thoughts and actions. Our ears are attuned only to His voice, not the voice of mankind that has fallen. Our mouth only speaks what we hear the Father speak. Our movement is guided by the Spirit as we are bound to Christ. This description is the body of Christ. A transformed person who is identifying with Christ through their very being. The Lord says His righteousness will be seen and His Glory will be upon us. That Glory is the same Glory when Christ walked the earth after He rose out of the tomb. I've mentioned before that our body is a tomb, and we'll enter His glorious, immortal body beyond ourselves. Until this occurs, our identity as the body of Christ on earth transcends name or creed. When I pray, I know the words that proceed from my mouth are His words. When I speak His words, it's His body speaking. If it's His body, then we are all part of the body of Christ.

Don't forget, there are seven churches in the last days, and every person on earth is affiliated with one of those churches. The church without love, the lukewarm, the dead, the persecuted, the compromised church, the faithful, and the false prophet called Jezebel church. Over the years, I've used these churches to gauge which church I am in by asking God. I followed His example and became part of the faithful church. And that's my permanent location. So, the body of Christ can be found in all these places. His word reveals that He is pleased with only two of those churches. The persecuted church and the faithful church. The others are not on the same page, and He holds something against them.

On earth and in heaven, mankind embodies the living body of Christ. If Christ perceives us as finished, we should have faith to persist until the end. We are one body with many members. In His body, each of us has a distinct role to play. Even Judas had a part to play in the story. It was necessary for someone to betray our Lord. So, burdened by guilt, Judas chose to end his own life. I'm willing to bet we'll see him in heaven. Removing walls and boundaries will allow us to connect and see each other. Regardless of being Jew or gentile, we will be joined together in the same olive tree, becoming one tree. The Lord's last commandment to us is to love one another.

We are all His children. One body, many members!

Today, the Lord offers you the option to choose between life and death. In our programming, we consider birthdays, age, wrinkles, retirement, death, and funerals. All pertaining to electing death each day. If the Lord considers it His body, shouldn't we align ourselves with glorification, resurrection, and life? Moses, at 85 years old, was still regarded as youthful. Noah built a massive ark before passing away at the age of 950. Instead of dying, Elijah and Enoch were transported to heaven. Jesus Christ, after rising from the dead, walked on earth in a state of glorification. The way is not through pre-programmed thinking, which has been the narrative of the fallen man's mind. Today, the decision of life or death is in your hands. See beyond the narrative and adopt the Messiah's approach. That will dramatically impact your final result!

The Lord owns the earth and everything in it! Our purpose is not to live for ourselves, but to be the possession of our Lord God. Before coming to earth, I believe we all stood before God's throne and received our assignments. Remember, our eternal spirit endures beyond this temporary life. The Lord has the power to give and take life; earth is just a brief assignment on our journey. The throne would have revealed to us our family lineage and the trials we must overcome to align with our divine blueprint. Most people are unaware of the plan and never begin their journey. Some individuals squander their time on the to-do list. However, some individuals consider themselves safe after being born again. Others find solace in a church building, dedicating themselves to good works. And let's not forget about the evil ones. Oh boy, they're around!

The Lord intends to restore us to our perfect dwelling place with Him. It has been preached that perfection is unattainable in this life. That comment always shocked me. I sought perfection in my relationship with the Lord, knowing He will return to His unblemished bride. He also states that we should be perfect just as He is perfect. He doesn't describe it as the other side of the grave.

It's another case of man's interpretation of not aligning with the Lord's mind. There was also an interpretation of a rapture by many people. The idea of leaving non-believers behind while the righteous ascend to the clouds was misguided. The Lord I know is not like that. His plan revolves around the idea that no man should perish. This preaching promoted escapism, allowing them to avoid confronting their own human weaknesses.

I once asked the Lord why He created the earth, and this is His response. He claimed that the earth is a seed, and we are responsible for carrying it. Inside us are more seeds which can be scattered. Some of those seeds fall by the wayside and the birds come and devour them. Some seeds landed on thorns, which then grew and suffocated them. Other seeds fell on good soil and yielded their crop; some a hundred-fold, some sixty-fold, some thirty-fold. The parable explains that we are the seed planted by the Lord on His farm, earth. The seed within us has an ability to multiply. When the Lord's plan is finished, the earth will be rolled up like a scroll and returned to the Lord's universe as a good seed. According to God, your achievements on earth will have significance in heaven. It's not about achieving for yourself, but about the seed within you. Planting our seed in good soil could lead to us having our own planet to manage. That's pretty neat! I'm open to accepting that offer. It's important to plant your seeds in good soil. For this reason, they will acquire treasures in the heavenly realms.

The walls need to come down! Although I am moved with excitement when I catch a glimpse of God's work within some of the people in Christendom. I anticipate the day when God's people come together and truly recognise our oneness. If we embrace one another in Christ, these walls between the ones on the outside of Christendom would no longer exist. I had to demolish my own barriers to appreciate that the Lord accepts both ways, Christian and those who call themselves 'no name'. It's not a matter of one or the other. 'Do not neglect coming together' is the scripture frequently thrown at me. Unbeknownst to the people who throw around this scripture, those in Christ outside the walls have been regularly meeting, but not in the same way as going to church on Sunday.

We were placed outside the walls by the Lord for a purpose. Many people the Lord is trying to reach outside the walls would never have set foot in a church building. It was our job to connect with them wherever they were. The fact that we were not in a church building worked in our favour, not against us. I formed a bond with them based on their individual life experiences and where they were at in their walk. Rather than their affiliation with religion, church buildings, or titles. Christ was the focal point, and He remains as such. People often ask me - how were they discipled? I authored books and gifted them to everyone I cross paths with. We are planted by God, not by people.

People develop walls due to the lack of Christ-like respect they receive along their path in life. Others were informed that those outside the walls were incorrect and needed to enter the building for correction. As I continued my walk, I came across the seven churches and became aware of my own deficiencies that required correction. The age-old scripture "remove the plank from your own eye before focusing on the speck in your brother's eye" is applicable in this scenario. We should make it a habit to check with God before we judge one another. Just because someone isn't like you doesn't mean they are not like God. Let's love one another! The walls are within us. Let's come together without barriers. The scripture "don't forsake the gathering" will be fulfilled by us coming together. My prayer is that those inside Christian walls and those outside the walls would be united as one body. No walls are unity in Christ.

Expanding on the individuals beyond Christendom's borders. I was in the desert for a while, as directed by the Lord. He brought a fellow along who was furious enough to crush beer cans with his bare hand. If the Lord hadn't intervened, he would have perished in the desert. Nowadays, this individual has developed a profound love for Jesus Christ, after fourteen years of knowing him. I've never met someone with more trauma than this person. His detachment from birth was a significant factor. This man's journey highlights God's faithfulness to orphans. I witnessed God's extraordinary efforts to bring this man to Himself, using the trauma as healing and someone like me on the outside of the walls to just loved him where he was at. There are many people who have no interest in entering a church building, and this person is one of them. The act of sitting and connecting with people is seen as a reflection of God's love. If the Titanic were sinking, this man would tear the door off and give it to me because I've taken the time to listen and be there for him when he needed it most. Every time I see this man, I give him a hundred hugs, but I've never received one of those hugs returned in fourteen years. Those who have been disconnected and not nurtured struggle to respond to love. Yet, he understands that God loves him, and that's extraordinary.

These individuals are strong and tender, happy to be who they have become without others around them. I didn't try to drag him into a church building; I just allowed God's plan for him to unfold. From a fallen man, this man healed me because he was so tough. I used to run a motel complex with homeless men, but this man was tougher than all of them. It has been said that if a woman led a man out of the garden, it should be a woman who leads him back in. On many levels, this man symbolises Adam. He's no longer angry. He's as gentle as a lamb nowadays.

Talking about the garden of Eden! While writing this passage, I had an amazing experience under a tree. I was sitting on the ground, with my arm on a chair, and a deadly brown snake suddenly rose up just inches away from my face. Our eyes met, and I'm unsure if my scream caused it, but the snake was forcefully pulled back by the power of that scream. It vanished from sight as it slithered into the magnificent ancient tree I was sitting beneath. I said to myself, Eve was yours six thousand years ago and I've been living with that mistake my whole life. I'm not falling into your trap again! It felt like the end of something old, and the beginning of something new. Our soul will eventually make its way back to God's garden if we've embraced that mantle. After completing four books of overcoming that day, I felt like the day my soul fully returned to say NO to that snake! Resist the devil and he will flee.

Job done!

Abundance of life awaits beyond the fallen tree! My friend stated, "Expect the unexpected." People often pray for abundance, but for me, the true abundance lies in peace, joy, and freedom in Our Lord. It's not about possessions or material items. Our journey through the depths of our soul will give life to this scripture.

Many individuals think they are doing well in life, and some even believe they are coming out on top.

Yet, it is nothing more than an illusion from the tree of knowledge of good and evil. The individuals who are aware of their position in His Kingdom are running last in the world system. They will be elevated by the Lord's hand in the days ahead. The new government on earth will be ruled by them and our Lord as one. Instead of ruling over, this new leadership will collaborate and march side by side. In past leadership, leaders were elevated as the top authority, and we were expected to unquestioningly follow regulated ways. There is a divide in that particular leadership style. The new leadership will respect each other and value our unique gifts and talents. A gathering without divisions! The head role will not be given to any one person; instead, we will stand united under the Lord's leadership and headship.

I encountered a man whose face reflected Jesus Christ. The inside of this man had undergone a transformation, becoming a new being. Those individuals will be the ones leading the next era of God's rule on earth. He has become what is rarely witnessed in another person - transformed. Many are called, few are chosen. This man is one of the chosen ones. The Lord calls us by name. Did you hear the call? By the Spirit, you will recognise them. I hope he saw in me what I saw in him, united as the body of Christ, working together to bring the Lord's vision to the earth. With God, all things are possible.

Picture a world where man and God coexist as a single entity on earth! My heart is filled with joy at the thought. Upon meeting Jesus Christ, I made a commitment to follow Him to the ends of the earth, no matter what it took. He said to me, "I want to give you the nations and the ends of the earth as your possession." You can't outdo our Lord! Whatever you give is only a portion of what He gives back. Renouncing the darkness within me set me free to embrace my true identity.

A lot of individuals hesitate to enter the process of overcoming. You come out emanating joy, freedom, wisdom, peace, rest, and purpose in life. I managed to stay upright on the narrow path, even with a snake in my face. I had a background in business before embarking on the overcoming walk - encountering both the compromised and loveless churches. It takes a while to rectify the abuse of the heathen life before Christ. However, the journey is worth it! My first encounter with Jesus Christ was face to face. It completely turned my life around. Despite the passing of thirty years since we first met, my love for Him only grew stronger with time. Seeing His vision come to fruition on earth is something that sticks with you, and I have no intention of shaking it off. Through twelve years of solitude in a tent near rivers and under trees, He taught me faith and brought me past my fears. It repaired the compromise within me and transformed my mindset. I regained self-love because He loved me unconditionally. I can't help but feel and think of love for my fellow man nowadays. The Lord uncovered the secret to love. Abide in faith, hope, and love, but remember that love surpasses them all.

It's time to open our hearts to love! It's the key that turns all things around. Different from the way the hippies loved. They indulged in marijuana and had a pleasant slumber together. In the midst of a spiritual experience, the spirit present may not always be the one belonging to Jesus Christ.

We, who have become part of the Kingdom of God and have been trusted with the King's possessions, are members of His household. What belongs to Him is also ours. Our Lord's voice guides us to bring both the old and the new from the storehouse. "Build my house and I will build your house, says the Lord." For me, it's more than a partnership - it's a marriage.

The Kingdom of God is amongst us! With their heads in the clouds, people eagerly await the arrival of the Kingdom of God. As the Lord's words state, it is actually among us. There are individuals who have been transformed and are now carrying His presence on earth. The complete Glory and righteousness in these people have not been fully revealed by the Lord. The moment of revealing is almost here. The Kingdom of God is within both you and me, but how far have you come in overcoming your fallen nature to reveal the King of Glory? I'm convinced that another occurrence, similar to when the Holy Spirit came upon us, will happen. The Holy Spirit descended upon Jesus while being baptised by John. A hundred and twenty people in the upper room, accompanied by tongues of fire, were their manifestation. I experienced a cloud hovering over my bed and that cloud entered my body when I received the holy Spirit. The act of walking down the front of a church to be anointed by the Holy Spirit through the pastor's prayer has always made me doubtful. The Spirit did not always manifest, or am I missing something? The presence of the Holy Spirit on Jesus, the hundred and twenty and myself were all heavenly manifestations on earth. The revelation of His righteousness and glory will occur in those who have embraced the Kingdom of heaven within them. Earth will witness yet another manifestation. Like Jesus' resurrection from the tomb! "Greater things we will do," the Lord said.

When Jesus was with the disciples, they multiplied like seeds. The occurrence of multiplication has been present in all of mankind since the crucifixion. Throughout all generations, we have faithfully carried out the scripture's instruction to preach the Word worldwide. Many ministries were built upon the foundation of that scripture. The mantle has resulted in a lot of bloodshed and a lot of souls being presented to the Lord. What if that mandate is fully accomplished? Consider a scenario where the gospel has reached every tongue and tribe. What would happen if we moved into a season of reaping the harvest? A time is coming when the Holy Spirit will be poured out on everyone. Someone plants the seed, someone waters it, but only God can make it grow. Our Lord granted me a vision of the outpouring of the

Holy spirit. A cloud fell upon the minds of every man, woman, and child. The cloud infiltrated their minds, revealing the presence of the Lord God. After this experience, the majority of individuals shifted their focus and turned to our Lord. A few individuals chose not to alter their course and instead went back to their businesses or lifestyle.

My desert experience had some of those hardened people. It would require more than just my effort to guide them towards the Lord. They are individuals who possess a friendly yet tough nature. Out there, they have a saying: 'two goes out, one comes back'. If they have a dislike for you, they may choose to put you in a wombat hole. Indeed, tough individuals! People trying to escape often seek refuge in the remote corners of our nation to avoid detection. Usually, they have something big they are hiding. I heard their stories while standing around a fire with a few of those people. For the night, I became the confession box. There's no movie that can rival the tales I've heard in the outback desert. But I did see the Lord's love for them time and time again. And I've seen the Lord's love for me, warning me beforehand of dangerous situations.

To conclude this writing, I would like to share the revelation of the new thing the Lord is doing on earth. We are now moving into a different era, no longer focused on overcoming. Entering into "Behold, I am doing a new thing now, it springs forth, do you not see it?" I've noticed a shift in the atmosphere since the snake incident at the tree a few days ago. After speaking to my friend who has a prophetic edge, this is what was understood.

Over the course of our lives, we have witnessed several eras, including the industrial age, the technology and information age, and the Pentecostal age. Nevertheless, this era stands apart from the rest, for it is the age of Tabernacles. The Lord has rested His Glory on our shoulders and we are His tabernacle upon the earth. People who have been prepared by our Lord will impact someone's life through their words. It will have the effect of inspiration flowing from their mouth. By acting upon inspiration, the person will experience a seamless and speedy manifestation, free from hindrances. No added trouble! As our conversation progressed, we discovered that waiting on the Lord had brought about a pivot reminiscent of a ballerina. It has been reported that a ballerina at the highest level has acquired the skill of staying still inside herself while her body is in motion. That is the work the Lord has been doing to His body of Christ. As the next era of our Lord begins, we will remain still while our outside world moves swiftly. Those who are made ready by the Lord will speak, and the Lord's inspiration will flow and be established quickly, and your light shall shine upon the way.

During our conversation, I saw the scripture that discusses the trimming of your lamp. This lamp is us! Trimming is overcoming. The flame burning inside our body is the lamp. Christ in us the hope of glory. No one lights a lamp and puts it under a basket, but rather on a lampstand, and it gives light for all who are in the house.

Shine that light. You have been prepared for a time such as this!

# THE END

## and the START of something NEW!

*Diane Cordaire!*